The Big Book of Cyber Safety

Staying Safe Online

Amaara Verma & Abeer Verma

Fusion Books

Publisher : **Fusion Books**
X-30, Okhla Industrial Area, Phase-II
New Delhi-110020
Phone : 011- 40712200
E-mail : wecare@diamondbooks.in
Website : www.diamondbooks.in
Edition : 2026

Author's Note

We belong to a generation that has never known a world without the internet.

We study online.

We communicate online.

We build friendships online.

We create, learn, explore, and express ourselves in digital spaces every single day.

But while the internet gives us incredible opportunities, it also brings risks that many young users don't fully understand.

We wrote this book because cyber safety should not feel complicated, scary, or boring. It should feel empowering.

Young learners deserve to understand:

- How online systems work
- How digital risks happen
- How to protect themselves confidently
- How to use technology responsibly and ethically

Cyber safety is not just about avoiding danger.

It's about building awareness, resilience, and balance.

Through practical examples, real-life stories, simple explanations, and thoughtful reflections, this book aims to help students become not just tech users — but responsible digital citizens.

We hope this book becomes a guide, a classroom companion, and a conversation starter between students, teachers, and families.

The internet is powerful.

But informed minds are even more powerful.

— Abeer & Amara Verma

Preface

Children today are growing up in a deeply connected world. Smartphones, gaming platforms, messaging apps, social media, and online learning tools are part of everyday life.

However, alongside these opportunities, new challenges have emerged:

- Cyberbullying
- Online scams
- Identity theft
- Hacking
- Screen addiction
- Digital misinformation

Many young users encounter these issues before they are fully equipped to handle them.

The Big Book of Cyber Safety is designed as a structured, age-appropriate guide that introduces students to the digital world in a clear and relatable manner.

This book:

- Explains cyber crime in simple language
- Teaches safe password and device habits
- Encourages responsible social media use
- Introduces cyber laws that protect children
- Promotes healthy digital balance
- Provides real-world scenarios and action steps

Aligned with the spirit of NEP 2020 and 21st-century life skills, this book encourages critical thinking, ethical awareness, and digital responsibility.

Cyber safety is not a one-time lesson.
It is a lifelong habit.
By understanding risks early and developing strong digital habits, students can confidently navigate the online world with awareness and strength.

Foreword

We are raising the first truly digital generation.
Today's students are not just consumers of technology — they are creators, innovators, and future leaders in a connected world. Yet with digital access comes digital responsibility.

Cyber safety is no longer optional. It is foundational.
Just as children are taught road safety, health hygiene, and personal responsibility, **they must also be educated about:**

- Online behavior
- Data protection
- Digital rights
- Ethical tcchnology use
- Emotional wellbeing in virtual spaces

This book arrives at the right time — when digital exposure is increasing at younger ages.
By combining practical guidance with thoughtful reflection, Abeer and Amara Verma provide young readers with a balanced understanding of both the technical and emotional aspects of online life.
Their student-led perspective makes this book especially relatable and impactful.

The goal is not to create fear.
The goal is to create informed, confident, and ethical digital citizens.
In a world driven by technology, awareness is protection.
May this book inspire young readers to:
Be alert.
Be responsible.
Be balanced.
And most importantly — be kind online.

Table of Contents

Chapter 1

Let's Go Online!

The Digital World Around Us

Let's Begin

Riya is in Class 6. Every day after homework, she watches fun videos, chats with her friends, plays online games, and even attends coding classes online. She feels like the internet is a magic box—fun, fast, and full of surprises!

But one day, Riya received a message from a stranger offering a free game. She clicked the link—and her tablet stopped working!

What went wrong? Is the internet always safe?

Let's explore the online world and learn how to stay smart and secure.

Explore: What Is the Digital World?

The digital world includes everything we do using phones, computers, or the internet—watching videos, messaging friends, learning online, playing games, or using apps.

The internet is like a big online city:

- Websites are buildings with information
- Apps are shops or games you visit
- Chats are like talking to people at school or in the park

But just like real cities, not everything is safe. Some people can be rude, trick you, or steal things online. These are called **cyber threats.**

Why It's Important to Learn About Online Safety

As students, you are smart and tech-savvy. But being cyber smart means:

- Knowing when something online is suspicious
- Keeping your personal information safe
- Using digital tools responsibly

Let's understand how to enjoy the internet—without falling into trouble!

Digital Devices You Use Every Day

Device	Used For
Smartphone	Games, chats, apps, photos
Tablet	Learning apps, YouTube, drawing
Laptop/Computer	Schoolwork, email, research
Smart TV	Streaming shows, YouTube
Gaming Console	Online multiplayer games

All of these devices connect to the internet, which is why it's important to use them wisely.

Golden Rule:

If you won't do it in real life, don't do it online!
Would you talk to a stranger on the street? No. So don't reply to unknown people online either.

Try It!

Activity: Spot the Safe and Unsafe Actions

Circle the safe actions and cross the unsafe ones:

1. Sharing your school address on a game chat ✘
2. Telling your parents before installing a new app ✔
3. Using your name and age as a password ✘
4. Ignoring messages from strangers ✔
5. Clicking on a pop-up saying "You won!" ✘

Draw and Label:
Draw your favorite device and label the apps or websites you use the most. Circle the ones you think are educational and put a star next to the ones that are just for fun!

Think & Reflect

- Have you ever shared personal details online? Was it safe?
- If a stranger sent you a message, what would you do?
- Do you always check with a parent before downloading new things?

Let's Revise

✔ The internet is useful for learning, fun, and connection

✔ The digital world includes apps, websites, games, and more

✔ Always be careful of strangers, links, and unknown messages

✔ If something feels wrong—stop and tell an adult

✔ Be cyber smart, not just tech smart!

Check Yourself

1. What is the digital world?
A) A place where we do science experiments
B) Everything we do online using devices
C) A video game only for adults

✔ **Answer**: B

2. Which is the safest action online?
A) Clicking a pop-up gift offer
B) Telling your parents about a strange message
C) Sharing your photo with strangers

✔ **Answer**: B

3. Which of these is a digital device?
A) School bag
B) Bicycle
C) Laptop

✔ **Answer**: C

Cyber Smart Tip – Abeer
Before downloading any app, check three things:

1. Reviews
2. Developer name
3. Permissions requested

Smart users don't just install — they investigate.

Digital Balance Note – Amara
Technology is powerful — but your real world matters too.
Make sure screens don't replace conversations, hobbies, or outdoor time.

Beyond the Book

Mini Project: Cyber Safety Chart

Create a poster titled:
"5 Rules to Stay Safe Online"
Include drawings, examples, and tips. Hang it in your classroom or share it during assembly!

Digital Exploration:
Visit https://beinternetawesome.withgoogle.com with your teacher or parent and play the Interland game to learn internet safety while having fun!

Chapter 2

What Is Cyber Crime?

Trouble in the Online World

Let's Begin

Rohan loved making fun videos and sharing them with friends. One day, a stranger left a mean comment calling him names. Another day, someone sent him a link saying he could win free gaming points. He clicked it—and his phone started acting strange!

What happened to Rohan? Why do such things happen online? Welcome to the world of **cyber crime**—let's learn how it works and how we can protect ourselves.

Explore: Understanding Cyber Crime

Just like crimes happen in the real world (like stealing or bullying), some crimes happen in the digital world using the internet. These are called cyber crimes.

Cyber crime means any crime where a computer, smartphone, or internet is used to do something illegal or harmful.

Common Cyber Crimes That Affect Children

Cyber Crime	What It Means	Real-Life Example
Cyberbullying	Using the internet to tease, insult, or threaten someone	A classmate shares a meme mocking you
Phishing	Sending fake emails or messages to steal information	"Click here to win free game coins!"
Online Scams	Tricking people into paying money or giving personal data	A fake shop offers cheap phones but never delivers
Hacking	Breaking into someone's account or device	You're locked out of your gaming account
Impersonation	Pretending to be someone else online	Someone creates a fake Instagram profile with your name
Identity Theft	Stealing your personal details to misuse them	A stranger uses your name and address to order things
Doxxing	Sharing someone's private information online	Someone posts your phone number or address on social media

Why Are Kids Targeted?

- Kids are curious and trusting
- They may click on anything fun or colorful

- They don't always check with adults before sharing info
- They often use weak or easy-to-guess passwords

What Do Cyber Criminals Want?

They want:

- Your personal info (name, school, age, photos)
- Your passwords and accounts
- Your money or parents' money
- Your online identity to trick others

Try It!

Match the Term to Its Meaning

Term	Meaning
1. Cyberbullying	A. Fake message asking for personal details
2. Phishing	B. Pretending to be someone else
3. Impersonation	C. Mean messages or threats online

Answers: 1 → C, 2 → A, 3 → B

Think & Reflect

- Have you ever seen a strange message or fake ad online?
- Would you know if someone was pretending to be you online?
- How would you feel if someone shared your photo without asking?

Let's Revise

✔ Cyber crime is when someone does bad things using the internet

✔ It includes phishing, scams, cyberbullying, hacking, and more

✔ Kids are often targeted because they're less aware of the risks

✔ It's important to stay alert and talk to an adult if anything feels wrong

Check Yourself

1. What is phishing?
A) A fun online game
B) A trick to get your personal info
C) A way to block messages

✔ **Answer**: B

2. What should you do if you get bullied online?
A) Reply with mean words
B) Ignore it forever
C) Tell a trusted adult or teacher

✔ **Answer**: C

3. What is identity theft?
A) Stealing your lunch
B) Taking someone's name and personal info
C) Hacking a video game

✔ **Answer**: B

Cyber Smart Tip – Abeer
If a message creates urgency ("Act now!" "Last chance!"), pause. Scammers use pressure. Smart users use patience.

Digital Balance Note – Amara
Never blame yourself for being tricked.
The goal isn't perfection — it's learning and growing wiser.

Beyond the Book

Mini Project: Make a "Cyber Crime Detective" Chart

Create a chart that shows:

- The name of each cyber crime
- A symbol or drawing
- A short example

Display it in your school's computer lab!

Digital Exploration:

With your teacher, visit https://www.cybercrime.gov.in/ to see how people report cyber crimes in India.

Chapter 3

Types of Cyber Crime Kids Should Know

Let's Begin

Arnav was playing an online game when a message popped up: "Hey! I can give you unlimited game coins—just share your login password!"
He was excited—but his friend Meera stopped him. "That could be a trick!" she warned.

Was Meera right? What kinds of tricks happen online? Let's find out.

Explore: The Many Faces of Cyber Crime

Cyber crime isn't just one thing—it comes in many forms. Some are sneaky, some are scary, and some may even seem like fun at first.

Let's look at the most common types of cyber crimes that kids should know about—and how to avoid them.

1. Cyberbullying

Using the internet to hurt someone with mean comments, threats, or spreading lies.
Example: Someone sends you rude texts or posts your embarrassing photo.

✔ **What to Do:**
- Don't respond
- Take screenshots
- Tell a trusted adult or teacher

2. Phishing

Fake messages or emails that try to steal your info (like password, age, or phone number).
Example: "Click here to claim your free prize!"

✔ **What to Do:**
- Don't click on strange links
- Never share your personal details
- Ask an adult before filling out any forms

3. Hacking

When someone breaks into your device or account without permission.
Example: You suddenly can't access your game profile—it's been hacked!

✔ **What to Do:**

- Use strong, unique passwords
- Log out of shared computers
- Enable two-step verification

4. Impersonation

Pretending to be someone else online.
Example: A fake Instagram account with your name and photo.

✔ **What to Do:**

- Report it to the app/platform
- Tell your parents or teachers
- Never share too many personal photos

5. Online Scams

Tricking people into sending money or clicking fake offers.
Example: "Pay ₹10 and win an iPhone!"

✔ **What to Do:**

- Be smart—nothing is really free online
- Don't share card details or passwords
- Check websites carefully before using

6. Identity Theft

Someone steals your name, age, school, or photos to pretend to be you.
Example: A stranger signs up for contests or games using your information.

✔ **What to Do:**

- Don't overshare online
- Use nicknames in public games
- Use privacy settings on social media

7. Malware & Viruses

Harmful software that enters your device through downloads or clicks.
Example: You download a game from an unknown site, and your tablet slows down.

✔ **What to Do:**

- Never download from unknown sources
- Install antivirus protection
- Ask a parent before downloading anything

Try It!

Activity: Classify the Cyber Crime
Match the situation to the correct cyber crime.

Situation	Cyber Crime Type
Someone spreads false stories about you in a group	A. Phishing
A message asks for your gaming password	B. Identity Theft
Someone makes a fake Facebook profile in your name	C. Cyberbullying
You download a free game and your screen freezes	D. Hacking or Malware

Answers:

- 1 → C
- 2 → A
- 3 → B
- 4 → D

Think & Reflect

- Have you ever seen one of these cyber crimes happen to someone?
- Why do you think scammers use "free gifts" to trick people?
- Which of these crimes do you think is the most dangerous, and why?

Let's Revise

✔ Cyber crimes come in many forms—bullying, scams, identity theft, and more

✔ Kids are often tricked through games, chats, or links

✔ Think before you click or share

✔ Always talk to an adult if something seems wrong

Check Yourself

1. What is cyberbullying?

A) Playing a game together

B) Sending kind messages online

C) Using the internet to hurt someone

✔ **Answer**: C

2. What should you do if you see a scam message?

A) Share it with friends

B) Report it and tell an adult

C) Click to find out more

✔ **Answer**: B

3. What is malware?

A) A kind of music

B) A harmful software

C) A messaging app

✔ **Answer**: B

Cyber Smart Tip – Abeer

Use different passwords for games, school, and social media.
One leak should not unlock your entire digital life.

Digital Balance Note – Amara

Behind every screen is a real person.
Choose kindness — even when others don't.

Beyond the Book

Activity: Cyber Crime Comic Strip

Draw a 4-box comic showing a cyber crime (like phishing or hacking) and how a smart kid stops it.
Label each box: What Happened, The Mistake, What They Did, Lesson Learned

Bonus: Create a slogan for each cyber crime type:
"Think Before You Click!"
"My Password, My Secret!"
"Report. Block. Speak Up!"

Chapter 4

What Is Cyber Security?

Your Online Shield

Let's Begin

Imagine your house has a strong door, a lock, and a security camera. These things protect you and your family from danger.

Now think about your phone, tablet, or computer. Do they have locks too? How do you protect yourself online?

Welcome to the world of Cyber Security—the locks, shields, and rules that protect you in the digital world.

Explore: What Is Cyber Security?

Cyber security means protecting your:

- Devices (like phone, laptop)
- Data (like your name, school, photos)
- Accounts (like your game login, email, social media)

from cyber criminals, viruses, and hackers.
It includes habits and tools that keep your digital life safe—just like locking your front door at night.

Why Is Cyber Security Important for Kids?

You use the internet for:

- Studying
- Playing
- Watching
- Talking to friends

But without protection, your:

- Personal info can be stolen
- Devices can get damaged
- People can trick you

That's why cyber security is not just for adults—it's for you too!

Cyber Security Tools & Practices

Tool / Habit	Why It Matters
Strong Passwords	Keeps your account safe from hackers
Antivirus Software	Blocks harmful viruses and malware
Two-Factor Login	Adds extra safety when logging into accounts
Updates & Patches	Fix holes that hackers can use to break in
Privacy Settings	Controls who can see your posts, info, or activity

The 5 Golden Cyber Security Rules for Kids

1. Use Strong Passwords
Mix capital letters, numbers, and symbols
Example: P@ssw0rd2025!

2. Think Before You Click
If it looks too good to be true—it probably is.

3. Don't Overshare
Never post your home address, school name, or phone number online.

4. Update Your Apps and Devices
Keep them up to date to stay protected.

5. Log Out Every Time
Especially when using a shared or public computer.

Try It!

Activity: Spot the Safe Action
Mark ✔ for safe and ✘ for unsafe:

Action	Safe or Unsafe
Sharing your password with your best friend	✘
Using Myname123 as a password	✘
Installing antivirus software	✔
Clicking unknown links in a group chat	✘
Turning on two-step login for your email	✔

Think & Reflect

- Do you know all the passwords to your accounts? Are they strong?
- Do you click "remind me later" when an update shows up?
- Have you ever told someone your password?

Let's Revise

✔ Cyber security means protecting devices and data online
✔ It includes tools like passwords, antivirus, and privacy settings
✔ You must be careful with what you share and click
✔ Every kid can practice good cyber hygiene

Check Yourself

1. What is cyber security?
A) A game to play with friends
B) Protecting your online life from threats
C) A kind of computer virus
✔ **Answer**: B

2. Which of these is a good password?
A) 123456
B) Myname
C) M@nGo2024!
✔ **Answer**: C

3. Why should you log out of your account on public computers?
A) To save electricity
B) To protect your account from misuse
C) So your friends can use it
✔ **Answer**: B

Cyber Smart Tip – Abeer
Turn on two-factor authentication wherever possible.
It's like adding a second lock to your digital door.
Digital Balance Note – Amara
Security is not fear — it's self-respect.
Protecting your data means valuing yourself.

Beyond the Book

Cyber Shield Poster Project

Create a poster titled:
"5 Ways I Stay Safe Online"
Use drawings, stickers, or magazine cut-outs. Make it colorful and hang it in your school computer lab!

Ask at Home:

- Does your family use antivirus software?
- Do your parents know about two-step login?

Explore More:
Ask your teacher to help you search for:

- Cyber security games or quizzes
- Stories of how kids protected themselves online

Chapter 5

Hacking

The Good, The Bad, and The Ethical

Let's Begin

Sania's school website was down. The computer teacher explained that someone had hacked it and changed the homepage. Sania was shocked. "Isn't hacking bad?" she asked.
"Not always," said the teacher. "There are good hackers too!"
Wait—can hacking be good? Let's find out!

Explore: What Is Hacking?

Hacking means breaking into a computer, app, website, or system without permission. It can be used for bad reasons—but sometimes also for good!

Just like a key can be used by:

- A thief to enter a house **(bad)**

- A locksmith to fix a lock **(good)**

Hacking depends on who is doing it and why.

Three Types of Hackers

Hacker Type	What They Do	Symbol
Black Hat	Hackers who steal, destroy, or harm systems illegally	
White Hat	Ethical hackers who help protect systems and find bugs	
Grey Hat	Hackers who explore systems without bad intent—but still without permission	

What Is Ethical Hacking?

Ethical hackers use their skills to:
- Help companies find weaknesses in their systems
- Prevent real hackers from attacking
- Protect people's data and privacy

They often work with:
- Schools
- Governments
- Cybersecurity companies

✔ They always ask for permission and follow the law.

Dangers of Unethical Hacking

Problem	What Could Happen
Email Account Hacked	You lose access, private info is leaked
School System Breached	Marks or student data may be changed

Game Profile Hacked	Coins, levels, or friends may be lost
Device Taken Over	Someone spies on your messages or camera

Try It!

Activity: Hacker or Helper?

Label each character as:

- Black Hat (B)
- White Hat (W)
- Grey Hat (G)

1. Ravi breaks into a school server and deletes records. → ___
2. Aisha finds a bug in a bank's app and reports it. → ___
3. Tanmay explores his school Wi-Fi without permission, just for fun. → ___

Answers:

1 → B
2 → W
3 → G

Think & Reflect

- Would you want to learn how to hack—but for good?
- What makes an action ethical or unethical?
- Should kids learn how ethical hacking works?

Let's Revise

✔ Hacking means accessing a system without permission
✔ It can be bad (black hat) or good (white hat)
✔ Ethical hackers help protect people and systems
✔ Cyber laws protect us from harmful hackers

Check Yourself

1. What is ethical hacking?

A) Hacking a friend's game for fun

B) Breaking into a system to harm it

C) Using skills to fix and protect systems with permission

✔ **Answer**: C

2. What do black hat hackers do?

A) Help fix websites

B) Play fair games

C) Steal or damage data

✔ **Answer**: C

3. What's a simple rule of ethical hacking?

A) Never ask for permission

B) Hack secretly

C) Always ask for permission and follow rules

✔ **Answer**: C

Cyber Smart Tip – Abeer

Curiosity is powerful.

Use it to build and protect — not to break or invade.

Digital Balance Note – Amara

Skills become meaningful only when guided by ethics.

Beyond the Book

Mini Project: Create a Hacker Profile Card

Pick one type of hacker (black, white, grey). **Draw or paste a cartoon figure and fill in:**

- What they do
- Good or bad?
- Real-life example (from news or research)

Explore Further:

Ask your teacher to show a kid-friendly video on ethical hacking and careers in cybersecurity.

Challenge:
Make a class presentation on how ethical hackers protect banks, schools, or the government

Chapter 6

Cyberbullying

It's Not Just a Joke

Let's Begin

Tanya posted a dance video online. The next day, her inbox was full of mean comments:

- "You dance like a robot!"
- "You look funny!"
- "Stop embarrassing yourself!"

Tanya felt hurt, confused, and didn't want to go online again.
Was this just a joke? Or something more serious?
This is an example of cyberbullying, and it's more harmful than it seems.

Explore: What Is Cyberbullying?

Cyberbullying means using digital tools—like phones, computers, or social media—to hurt, tease, threaten, or embarrass someone.

It can happen through:

- Messages or texts
- Comments on posts or videos
- Sharing private photos without permission
- Creating fake profiles to make fun of someone

Cyberbullying is real bullying, even if it's done through a screen.

How Is It Different from Regular Bullying?

Bullying at School	Cyberbullying
Happens face-to-face	Happens through devices
Usually stops after school	Can happen 24/7
Seen by few people	Can go viral or be public
May leave physical marks	Leaves emotional scars

Types of Cyberbullying

Type	Example
Harassment	Sending repeated hurtful messages
Outing	Sharing someone's secret or private info online
Exclusion	Leaving someone out of online groups on purpose
Trolling	Posting mean or silly comments just to provoke a fight
Impersonation	Pretending to be someone else and causing trouble
Shaming	Sharing embarrassing photos or videos to make fun of someone

Why Do People Cyberbully?

- To feel powerful
- To get attention or likes
- Because they are jealous
- Sometimes they are bullied themselves

But none of these are excuses. Hurting others is never okay—online or offline.

What to Do If You Are Cyberbullied

Step	Action
Don't Respond	Stay calm. Don't fight back or reply harshly.
Save Evidence	Take screenshots of the messages or posts.
Block the Bully	Use app settings to block or mute them.
Report It	Most platforms let you report bad behavior.
Talk to Adults	Share it with parents, teachers, or school head

Try It!

Activity: Is it Cyberbullying?
Mark ✔ if it's cyberbullying and ✘ if it's not:

Situation	✘ / ✔
A friend calls you a silly name once as a joke	✘
Someone posts your photo without asking and mocks it	✔
You politely disagree with someone's opinion	✘
A classmate keeps sending you rude DMs even when asked to stop	✔

Think & Reflect

- Have you ever witnessed cyberbullying online?
- Did you speak up or stay silent? Why?
- What would you do differently next time?

Let's Revise

✔ Cyberbullying is bullying through phones, apps, or the internet
✔ It includes teasing, threatening, excluding, or embarrassing others
✔ It can hurt deeply and stay online forever
✔ Always report, block, and talk to a trusted adult if it happens
✔ Be kind and respectful online—your words matter!

Check Yourself

1. Which of these is a form of cyberbullying?
A) Saying "Good job!" in a comment
B) Posting someone's secret online
C) Playing games online
✔ **Answer**: B

2. What should you do first if you're cyberbullied?
A) Reply and argue back
B) Save the messages as proof
C) Delete your account
✔ **Answer**: B

3. What's the best way to stop cyberbullying in class?
A) Ignore it and hope it goes away
B) Join the bully to be cool
C) Speak up and support the victim
✔ **Answer**: C

Cyber Smart Tip – Abeer
Save evidence. Block. Report. Tell an adult.
Silence protects bullies — action protects you.
Digital Balance Note – Amara
If someone hurts you online, it says more about them than about you.

Beyond the Book

Kindness Challenge

Start a week-long kindness campaign in your class:

- Post one kind message a day
- Create a "Kind Online Wall"
- Write anonymous compliments for classmates

Role-Play Game

Act out cyberbullying scenarios in small groups. One student is the bully, one the victim, and others are helpers or bystanders.

Then, discuss:

- What went wrong?
- What could have been done better?

Chapter 7

Online Scams and Fake Messages

Don't Fall for It!

Let's Begin

Ishaan got an exciting message on his game app:
"You've won 10,000 diamonds! Click here to claim your prize!"

He clicked the link—and suddenly, the app closed, his phone froze, and strange ads started popping up.

Ishaan had just fallen for an online scam.
What are scams? Why do they happen? How can we spot and stop them?

Explore: What Are Online Scams?

An online scam is when someone tricks you into giving personal information or money using fake messages, offers, or websites.

Scammers try to make their messages look:

- Very exciting or scary
- Like they are from real companies
- Like they need your quick action

They may come through:

- SMS
- Emails
- Game or app notifications
- Social media DMs
- Pop-up ads

Common Online Scams Children Face

Scam Type	What It Says	The Trick
Fake Prize Alerts	"You won ₹10,000! Click here!"	Steals your data or installs viruses
Free Game Coins	"Get unlimited diamonds now!"	Asks for account login or payment
Fake App Downloads	"New cool game! Download now!"	Infects device with malware
Fake Charity Scams	"Donate to help poor children today!"	Steals money through UPI or card fraud
Scare Messages	"Your account will be deleted in 1 hour!"	Pushes you to give details in a hurry

Red Flags – Spot the Scam!

- Too good to be true? It's probably fake.
- Bad grammar or spelling? Could be a scammer.
- Urgent message with fear or greed? Stay calm, don't act fast.

- Asking for money or passwords? NEVER share.
- Unknown links? Don't click!

What To Do When You See a Scam

1. Don't Click

Ignore or delete suspicious messages.

2. Don't Share Info

Never enter your name, age, school, or passwords.

3. Block & Report

Use app or website tools to report scams.

4. Tell a Trusted Adult

Share it with parents, teachers, or guardians immediately.

Try It!

Activity: Scam or Not?

Circle ✔ if it's a scam, ✘ if it's safe:

Message ✔ / ✘

"You won ₹1 lakh! Send your bank details now." ✔
Your teacher emails you homework on your school ID. ✘
A pop-up says "Download this antivirus to clean your phone."✔
A friend asks for help with a school project. ✘

Think & Reflect

- Have you ever received a scam message or fake pop-up?
- What would you do if a friend shares a suspicious link?
- Why do you think people fall for fake prizes?

Let's Revise

✔ Online scams trick you into sharing personal data or money
✔ They often use fake prizes, scary messages, or free offers
✔ Be alert, think before you click, and never act in a hurry
✔ Report scams and always ask a trusted adult for help

Check Yourself

1. What is a sign of an online scam?
A) A kind message from your classmate
B) A message with spelling errors and fake prizes
C) A school notice on your class group
✔ **Answer**: B

2. What should you do when you see a suspicious link?
A) Click to check what it is
B) Send it to all your friends
C) Don't click and tell an adult
✔ **Answer**: C

3. Why do scammers make messages urgent?
A) So you stay calm
B) So you take your time
C) So you panic and act fast without thinking
✔ **Answer**: C

Cyber Smart Tip – Abeer
Nothing online is truly "free."
If money isn't involved, your data might be.
Digital Balance Note – Amara
Excitement can cloud judgment.
Slow decisions are often smarter decisions.

Beyond the Book

Create a **"Scam Watch"** Wall

With your classmates, design a wall chart of:

- Common scam tricks
- Visual examples (drawn or printed)
- What to do if you see one

Classroom Game: Spot the Scam

Your teacher reads out short messages. Students raise a red card for scam and green for safe. Then explain why!

Chapter 8

Smart Social Media Use

Be Seen, Be Safe

Let's Begin

Simran just turned 13 and created her first Instagram account. She posted photos of her birthday party. The next day, she had 50 new followers—some were strangers.

One person messaged her:
"Hey! You're so cool! Want to be friends?"
Should she reply? Is it safe?
Social media can be exciting—but also tricky.
Let's learn how to stay smart on social platforms!

Explore: What Is Social Media?

Social media includes websites and apps where people:

- Share photos or videos

- Chat and comment
- Post opinions or updates
- Join groups and trends

Popular platforms for kids and teens:
- Instagram
- WhatsApp
- YouTube
- Snapchat
- Discord

These platforms connect us—but we must use them wisely and safely.

Smart Social Media Habits

Do	Don't
Use a private account	Use your full name in public profiles
Share posts with friends only	Post your home address or school name
Think before you post	Post when angry or upset
Block/report rude people	Chat with strangers or reply to unknown messages
Get parent/guardian permission before signing up	Believe everything you see online

Privacy Settings Matter!

Always:
- Turn on privacy in settings (only friends can see your posts)
- Disable location sharing
- Avoid using your real birthday, phone, or address online

Even with friends, remember:

Once posted = Always online

What Not to Post

- Home photos showing your address or room details
- Daily routine (like when you're home alone)
- Photos of others without permission
- Screenshots of private messages
- Hurtful or mean comments

Rule: *If you wouldn't say it face-to-face, don't post it online.*

What Can Go Wrong?

Wrong Action	Possible Result
Posting publicly without privacy settings	Strangers can see and misuse your content
Accepting friend requests from strangers	They may be fake or dangerous
Sharing your photo in school uniform	Your location or school identity becomes known
Commenting rudely on others' posts	Could lead to cyberbullying or account reporting

Try It!

Safe or Unsafe? Mark ✔ or ✘

Social Media Activity ✔ / ✘
Using a cartoon as your profile picture ✔
Posting your vacation location while you're still there. ✘
Accepting only people you know as followers ✔
Sharing your school ID card in a story ✘

Think & Reflect

- Why do people post so much about themselves online?
- Have you ever posted something you later deleted? Why?
- How can you make social media a kinder place?

Let's Revise

✔ Social media connects us but also needs careful use

✔ Always keep accounts private and avoid oversharing

✔ Be respectful and kind—your words matter

✔ Think before you post: Is it true, kind, and necessary?

✔ If you feel uncomfortable online, talk to an adult

Check Yourself

1. What is a good rule for social media posting?

A) Share every detail of your day

B) Post without checking your settings

C) Think before you post and protect your privacy

✔ **Answer**: C

2. What should you do if someone sends you a strange message?

A) Reply quickly

B) Block and report

C) Add them as a friend

✔ **Answer**: B

3. Is it safe to post your school name and location online?

A) Yes, it's fun

B) No, it reveals personal information

C) Only on weekends

✔ **Answer**: B

Cyber Smart Tip – Abeer
Private account > Public attention.
Security beats popularity.
Digital Balance Note – Amara
Likes fade.
Reputation lasts.

Beyond the Book

Create Your Social Media Safety Poster

Design a poster with:

- 3 Smart Things To Do
- 3 Things Never To Do
- A catchy slogan:

"Think Twice, Post Once!" or "Private is Powerful!"

Classroom Roleplay

Act out a social media scenario:

- One student posts something
- Others react as friends, strangers, or the teacher

Then discuss:

- What was good?
- What should be avoided?

Chapter 9

Strong Passwords & Safe Devices

Lock It Before You Lose It

Let's Begin

Rudra was locked out of his gaming account. Someone had guessed his password—**rudra123**—and changed everything.

He lost all his game progress.

"Why didn't I use a stronger password?" he wondered.

Just like your school bag has a zip, your **online world needs a lock too.** Let's learn how.

Explore: Why Passwords Matter

Your password is like the key to your digital house.
A weak password = an open door for hackers.

A strong password = a strong lock that protects your personal world.

You need passwords for:

- Email
- Games
- Social media
- Online learning apps
- Devices like phones or laptops

What Makes a Strong Password?

✔ At least 8 characters

✔ Mix of UPPERCASE, lowercase, numbers, and symbols

✔ Not your name, birthday, or pet's name

✔ Easy to remember, hard to guess

Examples of Strong Passwords:

- R@inbow7Tree!
- ZooFun_89#
- Mango4$Ever

Weak Passwords:

- password
- 123456
- myname123
- abcd

Password Safety Tips

Do	Don't
Change your passwords often	Use the same password everywhere
Keep your passwords private	Share your password—even with friends

Use different passwords for each app	Write them on your notebook
Use password manager apps (with help)	Reuse old or easy passwords

Device Safety Rules

Just like passwords, your devices need protection too!

Tips for Safe Devices:

- Use a screen lock (PIN, pattern, or fingerprint)
- Never leave your device unlocked and unattended
- Install antivirus protection
- Keep apps and software updated
- Don’t connect to unknown Wi-Fi networks

Try It!

Activity: Strong or Weak?

Mark ✔ if the password is strong, ✘ if weak:

Password ✔ / ✘

cat123 ✘

P@ndaRocks89! ✔

yourname2008 ✘

H0tChoco$un ✔

Think & Reflect

- Do you use the same password everywhere?
- Have you shared your password with someone before? Why?
- What would happen if your school ID password was hacked?

Let's Revise

✔ Passwords protect your accounts like a lock
✔ Strong passwords mix letters, numbers, and symbols
✔ Never share your passwords—not even with friends
✔ Keep devices locked, updated, and virus-free
✔ Treat your password like a toothbrush: don't share it!

Check Yourself

1. What is a strong password made of?
A) Only your name
B) A mix of letters, numbers, and symbols
C) Your favorite fruit
✔ **Answer**: B

2. What should you never do with your password?
A) Share it with your best friend
B) Change it regularly
C) Keep it private
✔ **Answer**: A

3. Which of these is a good device safety rule?
A) Leave your phone unlocked at school
B) Always update your apps
C) Write your passwords on your school desk
✔ **Answer**: B

Cyber Smart Tip – Abeer
Treat passwords like toothbrushes:
Don't share them. Change them regularly.
Digital Balance Note – Amara
Trust is important — but boundaries are powerful.

Beyond the Book

Design Your Own "Super Password" Shield

Draw a shield and write:

- Your password tips
- 2 sample strong passwords
- A safety slogan:

"Passwords Protect You!" or
"Lock It or Lose It!"

Home Task: Tech Safety Check

With your parents, check:

- Are your devices locked?
- Are your apps up to date?
- Are your passwords strong and unique?

Chapter 10

What To Do If Something Goes Wrong

Speak Up, Stay Safe

Let's Begin

Naina got a strange message from an unknown user:
"I know where you live. Send me a photo or I'll tell your parents you've been chatting with strangers!"
Naina felt scared and confused. She didn't know what to do.

Many kids feel the same way when something goes wrong online.
But there's a way out—always.
Let's learn what to do when things go wrong in the digital world.

Explore: Signs Something's Not Right Online

Sometimes, the internet feels uncomfortable or even scary. That's when it's time to take quick, smart action.

Red Flag	What It Might Mean
A stranger keeps messaging or threatening you	Cyberstalking or blackmail
You clicked a link and your device froze	Virus or malware attack
You're being teased or bullied online	Cyberbullying
Someone posted your photo without permission	Privacy breach or impersonation
You feel scared, anxious, or uncomfortable	Emotional impact of online activity

What To Do – Step by Step

1. Stay Calm
Breathe. Don't panic. You are not alone.

2. Don't Delete Anything
Take screenshots of messages or posts—this is evidence.

3. Tell a Trusted Adult Immediately
A parent, teacher, or school counselor can help.

4. Report and Block
Every platform has options to block and report users.

5. Avoid Responding to Threats
Don't argue or reply. It might make things worse.

6. Change Your Passwords
If your account was hacked or misused.

Who Can Help?

Helper	How They Support You
Parents/Guardians	Help you stay emotionally safe and act fast
Teachers	Can escalate issues within the school
School Counselors	Listen to you, support mental health
Police/Cyber Cells	Can investigate serious threats or crimes

In India, you can also call Childline 1098 or report at www.cybercrime.gov.in

Know Your Rights

Under India's IT Act & POCSO Act:

- No one can share your photos without permission
- No one can bully or threaten you online
- No one can ask a child for private or inappropriate content

These actions are punishable crimes

Try It!

Which Action Is Correct? (Tick ✔ the right response)

Situation	Action
A classmate keeps teasing you in a group chat	? Tell your teacher or parent
You clicked a suspicious link and now your phone is glitchy	? Inform a parent and scan the device
You feel scared about an online message	? Keep it secret / Share with an adult
Someone sends you a threatening photo	? Reply with your own / Take a screenshot + report

Answer: Always tell an adult, save proof, and never respond alone.

Think & Reflect

- Have you ever been in a situation where you didn't know what to do online?
- Why is it sometimes hard to ask for help?
- How can we make it easier for our friends to speak up too?

Let's Revise

✔ If something goes wrong online, don't panic—act smart
✔ Tell a trusted adult immediately
✔ Take screenshots of bad messages or posts
✔ Report and block the person or content
✔ Your safety comes first—you have the right to be safe online

Check Yourself

1. What should you do if someone sends you a scary message?
A) Reply angrily
B) Block and report, then tell an adult
C) Keep it secret
✔ **Answer**: B

2. Why should you save messages or screenshots?
A) To scare the bully
B) To delete later
C) To keep evidence for reporting
✔ **Answer**: C

3. Who can you contact in India for help with online crimes?
A) A gaming app
B) Cybercrime.gov.in or Childline 1098

C) Social media followers

✔ **Answer**: B

Cyber Smart Tip – Abeer
Screenshots are evidence.
Evidence creates solutions.

Digital Balance Note – Amara
Asking for help is not weakness.
It's courage.

Beyond the Book

Act It Out: Cyber Trouble Help Desk

In groups of 4:

- One child is the victim
- One is the bully/stranger
- One is the helper
- One is the teacher/parent

Perform short skits showing:

- What went wrong
- What the child should do
- How adults help resolve the problem

Classroom Poster Wall

Create posters with messages like:

- "Speak Up, Stay Safe"
- "Don't Suffer in Silence"
- "Save, Block, Report!"

Chapter 11

Laws That Protect You Online

Know Your Digital Rights

Let's Begin

Aarav was being bullied online by an older teen. He thought,
"There's nothing I can do. No one will listen to me."
But his teacher said,
"Aarav, you're protected by law. What happened to you is a crime—and you have the right to report it."
Yes, even kids have digital rights—and there are laws to keep them safe.
Let's understand the rules that protect YOU online!

Explore: What Are Cyber Laws?

Cyber laws are rules made by the government to:

- Protect people from crimes online
- Punish those who misuse the internet
- Keep children safe from bullying, threats, and harm

Just like there are traffic rules to keep roads safe, there are cyber laws to make the internet a safer space.

Laws That Protect Children Online (India)

Law	What It Does
Information Technology (IT) Act, 2000	Stops hacking, data theft, cyber bullying, online threats
POCSO Act, 2012	Protects children from online sexual abuse, grooming, and inappropriate content
Right to Privacy (Article 21)	Keeps your personal info private—no one can share it without permission
Juvenile Justice Act	Handles crimes by or against children, including cyber-related offenses

Your Online Rights as a Child

✔ **Right to Be Safe** – No one should threaten, harass, or abuse you online

✔ **Right to Privacy** – Your photos, videos, and info cannot be shared without permission

✔ **Right to Say No** – You can say no to anyone asking for personal details or images

✔ **Right to Report** – You can report any online threat to trusted adults or cyber police

Reportable Online Crimes (Even for Kids!)

- Cyberbullying
- Threats or blackmail
- Sharing of private photos without consent
- Inappropriate messages or content
- Fake profiles using your name or image
- Online grooming or strangers asking for personal info

These are not "mistakes" — they are crimes.

How to Report an Online Crime

1. Talk to a trusted adult
2. Collect evidence (screenshots, links, usernames)

3. File a report on:
www.cybercrime.gov.in
Or call Childline 1098

4. Report on the app or website (Instagram, YouTube, WhatsApp)

You can also file a report **anonymously** (without giving your name) for your safety.

Try It!

What Law or Right Applies? Match Them!

Situation	Law or Right
Someone posts your photo without asking	Right to Privacy
A stranger sends you inappropriate messages	POCSO Act
You report cyberbullying on the school website	Right to Report

Someone hacks your account and changes your info	IT Act

Answers: 1→ Right to Privacy, 2→ POCSO, 3→ Right to Report, 4→ IT Act

Think & Reflect

- Why is it important to know your rights online?
- How can these laws help you feel more confident online?
- What should you do if someone you know is afraid to report a cyber crime?

Let's Revise

✔ Cyber laws protect kids from online crimes
✔ IT Act, POCSO Act, and the Right to Privacy help keep you safe
✔ You have the right to say NO, block, and report
✔ You can file a report online or through trusted adults
✔ Laws are there to protect—not punish—innocent users like you

Check Yourself

1. What does the POCSO Act protect children from?
A) Road accidents
B) Online games
C) Online abuse and inappropriate content
✔ **Answer**: C

2. Can someone post your photo online without your permission?
A) Yes, it's just a photo
B) No, that breaks your right to privacy
C) Only if it's funny
✔ **Answer**: B

3. Where can you report cyber crimes in India?

A) Social media DMs

B) www.cybercrime.gov.in or Childline 1098

C) School WhatsApp group

✔ **Answer**: B

Cyber Smart Tip – Abeer

Know your rights. Knowledge is your strongest firewall.

Digital Balance Note – Amara

Laws protect dignity — yours and everyone else's.

Beyond the Book

Mini Project: Create a "Digital Rights for Kids" Scroll

On a long sheet, write down:

- 5 rights every child has online
- 3 examples of online crimes
- Where to go for help

Classroom Debate

Topic:

"Should children learn about cyber laws in school?"

Form two teams—For and Against.

Let each team speak, then vote as a class.

Chapter 12

Real-Life Cyber Stories of Kids

Learn from Their Mistakes

Let's Begin

Sometimes, we learn best from stories—especially when they're real. In this chapter, you'll meet kids like you who faced problems online. Some made mistakes. Some acted smart. All had something to teach.

Let's read, reflect, and remember:
Cyber safety isn't just theory—it's real.

Story 1: The Free Game Trap

Who: Ayaan, Class 6

What Happened:
Ayaan loved online games. One day, he saw a link:
"Unlock free skins for your character! Click here!"
He clicked it, entered his game login info, and… his account was stolen.

Lesson:

- Never click on unknown game links.
- Always check with a parent before logging into any site.
- Scammers often target kids through fake gaming offers.

Story 2: When Friendship Went Too Far

Who: Diya, Class 7

What Happened:

Diya became online friends with a boy named "Aryan." He seemed nice. But later, he asked for personal photos and threatened to share her chats if she didn't respond.

What Diya Did Right:

- She immediately told her mother
- They took screenshots and filed a complaint on cybercrime.gov.in
- Her parents blocked the user and reset her accounts

Lesson:

- Don't trust strangers, even if they seem kind
- Never share photos or personal info with online friends
- Always talk to a trusted adult when you feel uncomfortable

Story 3: The Class Group Bully

Who: Ishan, Class 8

What Happened:

A classmate started teasing Ishan in the school WhatsApp group.
"Your answers are always wrong!"
"Don't pretend to be smart."
The teasing turned into name-calling, and others joined in.

What Ishan Did:

- Took screenshots of the messages
- Shared them with his class teacher

• The school took action and educated the whole class on cyberbullying

Lesson:

• Don't stay silent—speak up against bullying
• Teachers and schools can help
• Hurtful words online are still bullying and must be stopped

Story 4: Password Problems

Who: Mehul, Class 5

What Happened:

Mehul shared his school email password with his best friend "just once." But soon, someone had sent silly messages from his account.

What Happened Next:

• Mehul's parents helped him change all his passwords
• His teacher reminded the class: Never share passwords—even with friends!

Lesson:

• Passwords are personal. Never share them.
• Use strong, unique passwords for every account

Reflect on These Stories

Ask yourself:

• Have I ever clicked a suspicious link?
• Do I talk to strangers online without knowing who they are?
• What would I do if I saw a classmate being bullied in a chat group?

Learning from others' mistakes helps us avoid making the same ones.

Let's Revise

✔ Real kids face real problems online—scams, bullying, strangers, and more
✔ In every case, telling a trusted adult helped solve the issue
✔ Your best tools are: awareness, quick action, and asking for help
✔ These stories show how being cyber smart makes a big difference

Check Yourself

1. What helped Diya get out of a scary situation?
A) Ignoring it
B) Arguing with the stranger
C) Telling her mom and reporting the user
✔ **Answer**: C

2. What did Ishan do when he was cyberbullied?
A) Fought back
B) Stayed quiet
C) Took screenshots and told his teacher
✔ **Answer**: C

3. What's the lesson from Mehul's story?
A) Change friends often
B) Sharing passwords can be risky
C) Jokes online are always fine
✔ **Answer**: B

Cyber Smart Tip – Abeer
Every mistake is data.
Learn from it. Upgrade your behavior.
Digital Balance Note – Amara
Growth begins when we reflect — not when we hide.

Beyond the Book

Class Skit Challenge

In groups of 4–5, act out one of the stories (or create your own) showing:

- What went wrong
- What the character did
- What others can learn from it

Cyber Story Comic Strip

Create a 4-panel comic strip showing one of the above stories with:

- A title
- Simple dialogues
- A moral message at the end

Chapter 13

The Future

Careers in Cyber Security

Let's Begin

Have you ever thought about becoming a superhero—not with a cape, but with a keyboard?

Meet Priya. She's 15 and loves solving puzzles and coding. She dreams of becoming an ethical hacker who helps protect banks from real hackers.

Sounds cool, right? That's the power of cyber security careers.

Explore: What Is a Career in Cyber Security?

A cyber security expert protects:

- People's data
- Bank systems
- Government websites
- Online apps and networks

They stop bad hackers, catch cybercriminals, and create safe systems for the digital world.
As more people use the internet, we need more cyber defenders!

Skills You Need to Start

You don't need to be a genius—you just need to be:
✔ Curious
✔ A good problem solver
✔ Honest and responsible
✔ Interested in tech and coding

Useful Subjects to Learn:
- Maths (logic, patterns)
- Computer Science (coding, networking)
- Ethics (right and wrong)
- Languages (for communication and research)

Future Cyber Jobs (Explained Simply)

Job Title	What They Do
Ethical Hacker	Tries to break systems—to find holes before bad hackers do
Security Analyst	Watches for threats and reports any danger
Cyber Forensic Expert	Investigates cyber crimes (like a detective!)
Malware Analyst	Studies harmful software to stop it from spreading
App Security Tester	Checks games and apps for bugs or weak spots
Privacy Officer	Helps companies protect people's private information

Where Can You Work?

- Banks and financial companies
- Hospitals and health tech
- Government offices (like Defence and Cyber Police)
- Big tech firms (like Google, Infosys, TCS)
- Schools and education startups
- Your own cyber safety startup!

Try It!

Match the Career to Its Work

Career	Work
Ethical Hacker	A. Studies how viruses spread on devices
Cyber Forensic Expert	B. Tries to break systems to test security
Malware Analyst	C. Solves online crime cases like a detective

Answers:
- Hacker → B
- Forensic → C
- Malware Analyst → A

Cool Cyber Projects You Can Start Now!

Join coding clubs or take beginner courses on:
- Scratch (block coding)
- Python or HTML (text coding)
- Cyber Safety workshops (like Google's Interland)

Take part in school quiz contests, cyber security days, or ethical hacking events for kids

Read books or comics about cyber heroes
Play games like Interland by Google to build cyber sense

Think & Reflect

- Would you like to solve online mysteries or build secure games?
- What excites you more: coding or catching criminals?
- Can you think of a cyber security problem you'd like to fix?

Let's Revise

✔ Cyber security is a growing field full of exciting jobs
✔ You can become an ethical hacker, forensic analyst, and more
✔ Start learning coding, problem-solving, and online safety now
✔ Every cyber hero starts small—with curiosity and courage!

Check Yourself

1. Who is an ethical hacker?
A) A hacker who steals money
B) A coder who helps stop crimes
C) A gamer who cheats
✔ **Answer**: B

2. What subject helps you become a cyber security expert?
A) Geography
B) Art
C) Computer Science
✔ **Answer**: C

3. Which job is like a detective?
A) Cyber Forensic Expert
B) App Designer

C) Password Maker

✔ **Answer**: A

Cyber Smart Tip – Abeer
Start early: coding + logic + curiosity = future-ready skills.

Digital Balance Note – Amara
Technology needs empathy as much as intelligence.

Beyond the Book

Make a Cyber Career Vision Board

Collect images or draw:

- Your dream tech job
- The tools you'd use
- A quote to inspire you

Add a title: "My Cyber Hero Future!"

Classroom Cyber Career Day

Invite a local cyber expert or parent in tech to talk to your class
Ask questions like:

- What do you do?
- How did you learn these skills?
- What advice do you have for kids?

Chapter 14

Digital Habits for a Healthy Life

Be Smart, Be Balanced

Let's Begin

Arnav wakes up and checks his phone.
He eats while watching YouTube.
He skips outdoor play to scroll Instagram.
He goes to bed with his tablet still glowing.
Sound familiar?
The internet is amazing—but if we don't use it mindfully, it can harm our health, time, and happiness.
Let's learn how to build healthy digital habits that keep us safe and happy.

Explore: What Are Digital Habits?

Digital habits are the things you regularly do online:

- How often you check your phone

- How much time you spend on games or videos
- How you feel when you're online—or offline

Healthy habits help your brain, body, and emotions.
Unhealthy ones can cause stress, sleep problems, or screen addiction.

Signs of Unhealthy Screen Time

Sign	What It Looks Like
Tired eyes	Headaches, itchy or dry eyes
Less physical activity	Not playing, exercising, or going outdoors
Losing focus	Daydreaming during class or homework
Mood swings	Feeling angry, bored, or sad when not online
Trouble sleeping	Going to bed late due to screens

How Much Screen Time Is Okay?

For ages 8–12:
Maximum 2 hours of non-educational screen time per day
Stop using screens at least 1 hour before bedtime
Take screen breaks every 30–40 minutes

Make time for offline fun: playing, reading, crafts, or talking with family

Good Digital Habits for Kids

Healthy Habit	Why It Matters
Take screen breaks	Gives your eyes and brain rest
Keep devices out of bed	Helps you sleep better
Use apps with purpose	Learn, explore—not just scroll

Spend more time outdoors	Keeps body and mind active
Talk face-to-face with people	Builds real friendships
Reflect before posting	Keeps your digital footprint clean and kind

Mindful Online Behavior

Before you post, ask:
T.H.I.N.K.

- T – Is it True?
- H – Is it Helpful?
- I – Is it Inspiring?
- N – Is it Necessary?
- K – Is it Kind?

If it's not all of the above—don't post it!

Try It!

Which Habit is Healthier? Circle the Better Choice

1. Watch YouTube while eating dinner OR Chat with family
2. Play outside for 1 hour OR Play mobile games alone
3. Keep your phone beside your pillow OR Keep it outside the room at night
4. Check notifications every 5 minutes OR Check your device 2–3 times a day

Think & Reflect

- How do you feel after spending too much time on screens?
- When do you enjoy life the most—online or offline?
- What's one screen habit you want to change this week?

Let's Revise

✔ Digital habits shape our health and happiness

✔ Too much screen time can hurt your eyes, mind, and mood

✔ Healthy habits include taking breaks, sleeping well, and staying active

✔ THINK before you post: True, Helpful, Inspiring, Necessary, Kind

✔ Enjoy the digital world—but don't forget the real world too!

Check Yourself

1. What is one sign of too much screen time?
A) Playing sports
B) Tired eyes and poor sleep
C) Laughing with friends
✔ **Answer**: B

2. What is a good bedtime habit?
A) Watch videos until you sleep
B) Use your phone under the blanket
C) Keep screens away 1 hour before sleep
✔ **Answer**: C

3. What does the "T" in THINK stand for?
A) Time
B) True
C) Talk
✔ **Answer**: B

Cyber Smart Tip – Abeer
Track your screen time for 3 days.
Measure first. Improve next.
Digital Balance Note – Amara
Balance is strength — not limitation.

Beyond the Book

Create a Personal Screen Time Tracker

Track your screen use for 3 days:

- How much time on school work
- How much on games/videos
- How much on chats

Then reflect:

- Which apps help me learn?
- Where can I cut back?
- What offline fun can I add?

Poster Project: Digital Balance is Beautiful

Design a half-and-half poster:

- One side shows a kid stuck to screens
- The other shows the same kid enjoying outdoor life

Caption it: *"Balance is Better!"*

Chapter 15

Project Time

Be a Cyber Safety Champion!

Let's Begin

Now that you've learned how to be smart, safe, and kind online...
It's time to put your knowledge into action!

This chapter helps you become a Cyber Safety Champion—someone who not only protects themselves but also helps others stay safe in the digital world.

Let's do this—together!

Explore: What Is a Cyber Safety Champion?

A Cyber Safety Champion is someone who:

- Practices good online habits every day
- Helps classmates or friends avoid online dangers

- Teaches others what they've learned about cyber safety
- Builds a safe, respectful, and kind online world

You don't need a badge or a certificate—your actions make you a real champion.

Final Cyber Skills Checklist

✔ I know what cyber crime is
✔ I can spot fake links or scam messages
✔ I protect my passwords and devices
✔ I report bullying or threats
✔ I THINK before I post
✔ I help my friends stay safe online

If you checked most or all of these… you're already on your way!

Project Activities

1. Design Your Cyber Safety Poster

Create a colorful poster with:
- 3 cyber safety tips
- 1 real-life scenario
- A powerful slogan like:

"Click with Care" or "Think Before You Share!"
Display it in your classroom or school library.

2. Give a Talk in Assembly

Prepare a 1-minute speech or role-play skit:
- **Topic ideas:** "Cyberbullying Isn't a Joke", "Be a Password Pro", or "Say No to Strangers Online"
- Include simple examples, do's and don'ts, and end with a catchy line

Ask your teacher for a chance to speak in front of your class or school!

3. Make a Cyber Safety Comic Strip

Create a 4-panel comic where:

- A problem happens online
- A smart kid takes the right steps
- A bully or scammer is stopped
- Everyone learns a lesson

Use speech bubbles and your own illustrations!

4. Start a 'Cyber Smart Club' at School

Form a team of 4–6 friends and plan monthly:

- Awareness days
- Poster competitions
- Quiz contests on digital safety
- Invite parents or teachers to share tips

Make your school cyber smart—one step at a time.

Check Yourself (Final Challenge Quiz!)

1. What's the first thing to do when something online feels wrong?

A) Keep it a secret
B) Report it and tell a trusted adult
C) Delete your account
✔ **Answer**: B

2. What is a Cyber Safety Champion?

A) Someone who plays games well
B) Someone who bullies bullies

C) Someone who helps others stay safe online

✔ **Answer**: C

3. Why should we THINK before posting?

A) To get more likes

B) To check if it's True, Helpful, Inspiring, Necessary, Kind

C) To be popular

✔ **Answer**: B

Cyber Smart Tip – Abeer

Teach one friend what you learned.

Security multiplies when shared.

Digital Balance Note – Amara

Leadership begins with responsibility.

Beyond the Book

Write a Pledge!

"I, ________, promise to be a Cyber Safety Champion.
I will stay alert, protect my privacy, and speak up when something's wrong.
I will use the internet with kindness and help others do the same."

Sign it, decorate it, and stick it on your wall!

You Did It!

You've reached the end of this book—but the journey has just begun.

Being cyber smart is not a one-time lesson—it's a lifelong habit.
Keep learning, stay alert, and help others in the digital world.

Glossary: Cyber Words You Should Know

Word	Meaning (Simple Definition)
Account	Your personal login to access websites, apps, or games.
Antivirus Software	A program that protects your device from harmful viruses.
App (Application)	A software tool or game you download to use on your device.
Block	A way to stop someone from contacting or messaging you online.
Cyberbullying	Using the internet to tease, threaten, or embarrass someone.
Cyber Crime	Any crime that happens using a computer or the internet.
Cyber Security	The tools and actions used to keep your online life safe.
Data	Information such as your name, photos, or passwords shared or stored online.
Digital Footprint	The trail of everything you do online—searches, posts, clicks.
Device	A gadget like a phone, tablet, or laptop that connects to the internet.
Ethical Hacker	A good hacker who helps find and fix online security problems.
Fake Link / Scam	A trick to steal your data or money by getting you to click something dangerous.
Hacker	A person who breaks into computers or networks—can be good or bad.
Impersonation	Pretending to be someone else online using fake names or photos.

Malware	Bad software that damages your device or steals information.
Password	A secret code you create to protect your online accounts.
Phishing	A fake email or message asking for personal details.
Privacy Settings	Controls that help you decide who sees your posts or info online.
Report	To inform the app or site that someone is doing something unsafe or wrong.
Scam	A trick to steal your information, money, or accounts.
Screen Time	The amount of time you spend on digital devices each day.
Social Media	Apps and websites where people share posts, photos, and messages.
Spam	Unwanted or junk messages sent in large numbers.
Stranger Danger (Online)	A warning about unknown people on the internet who may not be safe.
Strong Password	A hard-to-guess password with letters, numbers, and symbols.
Two-Factor Authentication	A second step (like a code on your phone) that keeps your account extra safe.